D1717086

VANESSA WILLIAMS

VANESSA WILLIAMS

❧

Suzanne Freedman

CHELSEA HOUSE PUBLISHERS
Philadelphia

This book is dedicated to Hila Colman, devoted friend and mentor,
who has consistently encouraged me in my writing career.

Chelsea House Publishers

Editor in Chief	Stephen Reginald
Production Manager	Pamela Loos
Director of Photography	Judy L. Hasday
Art Director	Sara Davis
Managing Editor	James D. Gallagher

Staff for VANESSA WILLIAMS

Prepared by	21st Century Publishing and Communications, Inc.
Contributing Editor	Anne Hill
Cover Illustration	Earl Parker
Cover Designer	Ian Varrassi, Keith Trego

The Chelsea House World Wide Web address is
http://www.chelseahouse.com

3 5 7 9 8 6 4 2
Library of Congress Cataloging-in-Publication Data

Freedman, Suzanne, 1932-
   Vanessa Williams / by Suzanne Freedman.
     100 pp.   cm. — (Black Americans of Achievement)
Includes bibliographical references and index.
Summary: A biography of the successful singer and actress who was
chosen as the first African American Miss America in 1983.
ISBN   0-7910-4959-0 (hc)
          0-7910-4960-4 (pb)
1. Williams, Vanessa—Juvenile literature. 2. Singers—United States—
Biography—Juvenile literature. 3. Actors—United States—
Biography—Juvenile literature. [1. Williams, Vanessa.
2. Singers. 3. Actors and actresses. 4. Women—Biography.]
I. Title. II. Series.
ML3930.W56F74   1999
782.42164'092—dc21
[B]   99-12390
                                                                              CIP
                                                                               AC

Frontis:
A talented and diverse artist,
Vanessa Williams has found
success in films, on the stage,
and as a recording artist.

CONTENTS

BLACK AMERICANS OF ACHIEVEMENT

HENRY AARON
baseball great

KAREEM ABDUL-JABBAR
basketball great

MUHAMMAD ALI
heavyweight champion

RICHARD ALLEN
religious leader and social activist

MAYA ANGELOU
author

LOUIS ARMSTRONG
musician

ARTHUR ASHE
tennis great

JOSEPHINE BAKER
entertainer

JAMES BALDWIN
author

TYRA BANKS
model

BENJAMIN BANNEKER
scientist and mathematician

COUNT BASIE
bandleader and composer

ANGELA BASSETT
actress

ROMARE BEARDEN
artist

HALLE BERRY
actress

MARY MCLEOD BETHUNE
educator

GEORGE WASHINGTON
CARVER
botanist

JOHNNIE COCHRAN
lawyer

SEAN "PUFFY" COMBS
music producer

BILL COSBY
entertainer

MILES DAVIS
musician

FREDERICK DOUGLASS
abolitionist editor

CHARLES DREW
physician

W. E. B. DU BOIS
scholar and activist

PAUL LAURENCE DUNBAR
poet

DUKE ELLINGTON
bandleader and composer

RALPH ELLISON
author

JULIUS ERVING
basketball great

LOUIS FARRAKHAN
political activist

ELLA FITZGERALD
singer

ARETHA FRANKLIN
entertainer

MORGAN FREEMAN
actor

MARCUS GARVEY
black nationalist leader

JOSH GIBSON
baseball great

WHOOPI GOLDBERG
entertainer

CUBA GOODING JR.
actor

ALEX HALEY
author

PRINCE HALL
social reformer

JIMI HENDRIX
musician

MATTHEW HENSON
explorer

GREGORY HINES
performer

BILLIE HOLIDAY
singer

LENA HORNE
entertainer

WHITNEY HOUSTON
singer and actress

LANGSTON HUGHES
poet

JANET JACKSON
musician

JESSE JACKSON
civil-rights leader and politician

MICHAEL JACKSON
entertainer

SAMUEL L. JACKSON
actor

T. D. JAKES
religious leader

JACK JOHNSON
heavyweight champion

MAGIC JOHNSON
basketball great

SCOTT JOPLIN
composer

BARBARA JORDAN
politician

MICHAEL JORDAN
basketball great

CORETTA SCOTT KING
civil-rights leader

MARTIN LUTHER KING, JR.
civil-rights leader

LEWIS LATIMER
scientist

SPIKE LEE
filmmaker

CARL LEWIS
champion athlete

JOE LOUIS
heavyweight champion

RONALD MCNAIR
astronaut

MALCOLM X
militant black leader

BOB MARLEY
musician

THURGOOD MARSHALL
Supreme Court justice

TERRY MCMILLAN
author

TONI MORRISON
author

ELIJAH MUHAMMAD
religious leader

EDDIE MURPHY
entertainer

JESSE OWENS
champion athlete

SATCHEL PAIGE
baseball great

CHARLIE PARKER
musician

ROSA PARKS
civil-rights leader

COLIN POWELL
military leader

PAUL ROBESON
singer and actor

JACKIE ROBINSON
baseball great

CHRIS ROCK
comedian and actor

DIANA ROSS
entertainer

WILL SMITH
actor

WESLEY SNIPES
actor

CLARENCE THOMAS
Supreme Court justice

SOJOURNER TRUTH
antislavery activist

HARRIET TUBMAN
antislavery activist

NAT TURNER
slave revolt leader

TINA TURNER
entertainer

ALICE WALKER
author

MADAM C. J. WALKER
entrepreneur

BOOKER T. WASHINGTON
educator

DENZEL WASHINGTON
actor

J. C. WATTS
politician

VANESSA WILLIAMS
singer and actress

OPRAH WINFREY
entertainer

TIGER WOODS
golf star

RICHARD WRIGHT
author

ON
ACHIEVEMENT

— ✿ —

Coretta Scott King

Before you begin this book, I hope you will ask yourself what the word *excellence* means to you. I think it's a question we should all ask, and keep asking as we grow older and change. Because the truest answer to it should never change. When you think of excellence, perhaps you think of success at work; or of becoming wealthy; or meeting the right person, getting married, and having a good family life.

Those goals are worth striving for, but there is a better way to look at excellence. As Martin Luther King Jr. said in one of his last sermons, "I want you to be first in love. I want you to be first in moral excellence. I want you to be first in generosity. If you want to be important, wonderful. If you want to be great, wonderful. But recognize that he who is greatest among you shall be your servant."

My husband knew that the true meaning of achievement is service. When I met him, in 1952, he was already ordained as a Baptist minister and was working toward a doctoral degree at Boston University. I was studying at the New England Conservatory and dreamed of accomplishments in music. We married a year later, and after I graduated the following year we moved to Montgomery, Alabama. We didn't know it then, but our notions of achievement were about to undergo a dramatic change.

You may have read or heard about what happened next. What began with the boycott of a local bus line grew into a national crusade, and by the time he was assassinated in 1968 my husband had fashioned a black movement powerful enough to shatter forever the practice of racial segregation. What you may not have read about is where he learned to resist injustice without compromising his religious beliefs.

He adopted a strategy of nonviolence from a man of a different race, who lived in a different country and even practiced a different religion. The man was Mahatma Gandhi, the great leader of India, who devoted his life to serving humanity in the spirit of love and nonviolence. It was in these principles that Martin discovered his method for social reform. More than anything else, those two principles were the key to his achievements.

These books are about African Americans who served society through the excellence of their achievements. They form part of the rich history of black men and women in America—a history of stunning accomplishments in every field of human endeavor, from literature and art to science, industry, education, diplomacy, athletics, jurisprudence, even polar exploration.

Not all of the people in this history had the same ideals, but I think you will find that all of them had something in common. Like Martin Luther King Jr., they all decided to become "drum majors" and serve humanity. In that principle—whether it was expressed in books, inventions, or song—they found a goal and a guide outside themselves that showed them a way to serve others instead of living only for themselves.

Reading the stories of these courageous men and women not only helps us discover the principles that we will use to guide our own lives; it also teaches us about our black heritage and about America itself. It is crucial for us to know the heroes and heroines of our history and to realize that the price we paid in our struggle for equality in America was dear. But we must also understand that we have gotten as far as we have partly because America's democratic system and ideals made it possible.

We are still struggling with racism and prejudice. But the great men and women in this series are a tribute to the spirit of the country in which they have flourished. And that makes their stories special and worth knowing.

1

"MISS AMERICA, YOU'RE BEAUTIFUL"

❦

Overwhelming is the best word to describe the Atlantic City Convention Center. Located on the southeastern shore of New Jersey's popular beach resort, the Atlantic City Convention Center is an impressive 13 stories high, 675 feet long, and 351 feet wide. In the past it has been the site of indoor football games, horse racing, and ice shows, and throughout the year the spacious building hosts boat displays, home shows, and musical performances. But the Convention Center's most popular event occurs annually in mid-September: the Miss America Pageant.

Every year, each of the 50 states chooses a representative to compete in the Miss America Pageant. If the contestants are not overwhelmed by the size of the Convention Center or by their own preparations for the pageant, they may be overrun by reporters. Nearly 400 newspaper, magazine, radio, and television representatives cover the annual event. Before the pageant, contestants are interviewed and photographed; afterward, multiple press conferences are held with the new Miss America.

Adding to the flurry of excitement is another long-standing tradition of Pageant Week—the Boardwalk Parade. Held on Atlantic City's six-mile boardwalk on the Friday preceding the crowning of the new Miss America, it is considered the grandest

Poised and smiling, Vanessa Williams has just won the Miss America 1984 title to become the first African American to capture the crown and scepter. Vanessa's victory proved that racial barriers could be broken and that other young black women could achieve their dreams.

11

of beauty pageant parades. The two-hour event is televised, and each year about 100,000 people flock to Atlantic City to see the famous spectacle. Celebrities such as Tom Jones, Grace Kelly, and Marilyn Monroe have served as the parade's grand marshal over the years.

Although famous figures mingle with the crowd, floats swarm the boardwalk, and the music of bands fills the air, the real stars of parade night are the contestants, dressed in costumes representing their states. The ocean breeze blows, the lights from the Atlantic City casinos shine, and people cheer and wave. Some even run up to the cars to shake hands with a favorite pageant participant and wish her luck. All of the contestants feel butterflies inside, for each one knows that the next night—Saturday, the final night of the Miss America Pageant—could be the most special night of her life.

On Saturday, September 17, 1983, television cameras prepared to deliver the finals of the 63rd Miss America Pageant into millions of American homes. A capacity crowd of 25,000 people sat on metal bleachers in a semicircle around the famous 125-foot runway in the Convention Center, anxiously waiting for the show to begin.

With so many beautiful, poised, and talented women competing, the judges for this year's contest had a difficult decision ahead of them. The panel consisted of Miss America 1956 Marian McKnight, singer and entertainer Jerry Vale, photographer Chris Little, world-renowned singer Marguerite Piazza, noted dance instructor Jeanne Meixell, poet Rod McKuen, and business executives Tandy Rice and Lois Ernst. They were asked to pick the new Miss America based on her performance in a number of categories: talent (each contestant's score in this category was worth 40 percent of her total score), a personal interview (30 percent), stage personality in evening wear (15 percent), and physical fitness in a swimsuit (15 percent).

By Saturday night, the talent competition and interviews were complete, and the field of 50 had been narrowed first to 10 finalists, then to five: Miss Ohio Pamela Rigas, Miss Alabama Pam Battles, Miss New Jersey Suzette Charles, Miss New York Vanessa Williams, and Miss Mississippi Wanda Gayle Geddie. One of these five young women would become Miss America 1984, while the four runners-up would comprise her court of honor.

At 10 P.M., as the stage lights dimmed, Glenn Osser, music director of the pageant for the previous 28 years, conducted the Miss America orchestra,

Dressed in an array of costumes, Miss America contestants show off their talents by performing an opening number during the final night of the pageant.

As Miss New York, Vanessa Williams won both the swimsuit and talent competitions in the preliminaries. Encouraged by these triumphs, Vanessa felt she had a real chance to win the coveted Miss America title.

which played the theme song of the 1983 pageant, "Go For It All:"

> It's that time - again
> There's that mountain to climb again
> The challenge is there,
> The prize is yours if you dare
> And you know—yes, you know
> You're gonna go for it. Go for it - go for it all . . .

Master of ceremonies Gary Collins then sang to Debra Sue Maffett, Miss America 1983, as she walked down the runway for the last time to a standing ovation:

> Miss America you're beautiful
> You have added luster to a crown you wore . . .

There had been some speculation that an African American would win the title for the first time in the history of the contest. Pageant officials had confirmed that two of the African-American contestants had especially impressed them in their private interviews with the judges and in the talent competition. Suzette Charles, a 20-year-old professional singer from Mays Landing, was the hometown favorite, having grown up only about 17 miles from Atlantic City. She had belted out Barbra Streisand's hit "Kiss Me in the Rain" to place second in the talent competition. The woman who edged her out, 20-year-old Vanessa Williams, was also African American. Williams, a musical theater major in her sophomore year at Syracuse University in upstate New York, had sung a balladlike rendition of "Happy Days Are Here Again," the Democratic party's theme song from the Franklin D. Roosevelt era.

"It's going to be the year of the black Miss America," Maffett, the reigning Miss America, had predicted before the contest, but both Charles and Williams downplayed the race issue. "The pageant is a fair competition and [we] believe we have as good a chance as any woman here," they agreed.

Williams, however, was beginning to believe that she had a better chance than most. On the first night of the judging, Wednesday, September 14, she had won the swimsuit competition. On Friday, the 16th, she ranked first in the talent competition, narrowly easing past Suzette Charles to become the first African-American woman to win both.

During the six decades of the pageant's existence, only a dozen black contestants had even participated in the contest. The event had been restricted to whites until the late 1950s. In 1970 Miss Iowa Cheryl Browne was the first African-American contestant. Before 1983, no black woman had ever finished higher than Lencola Sullivan from Arkansas, who was fourth runner-up in 1980. "The day it happens in the Miss America Pageant," Albert Marks Jr., chairman of the pageant, told reporters, "I think it would be a piece of big news."

The night's most suspenseful moment was at hand for the five hopefuls. They tried to hide their nervousness and appeared confident and self-assured as the final scores were tallied. On stage, these beautiful women clutched each other's hands as they awaited the announcement that would change one of their lives forever. In addition to the crown and the intense publicity that comes with it, Miss America 1984 would receive a $25,000 scholarship or cash and could be expected to earn more than $100,000 in appearance fees during her reign.

As the envelope was handed to Gary Collins, an anticipatory silence filled the vast convention hall. He announced that Miss Ohio was fourth runner-up; third, Miss Mississippi; second, Miss Alabama; first runner-up, Miss New Jersey. "And our new Miss America is . . . MISS NEW YORK . . . VANESSA WILLIAMS!"

Wearing a lavender gown, Vanessa Williams glided to center stage. She embraced Debra Sue Maffett and paused to receive a glittering crown and a scepter

Leaping into the air on the beach at Atlantic City, an exuberant Vanessa displays the spirit, energy, and confidence that helped her win the Miss America title. Her education, hard work, and ambition also played a major role in her success.

adorned with roses. Vanessa then paraded down the runway as the new Miss America, saying simply "thank you so much" and smiling. At that moment, she was more than just Miss America. Vanessa Williams was the new symbol of American beauty, a standard that had traditionally excluded African Americans.

The 5'6", 110-pound, green-eyed brunette had dazzled the all-white panel of judges. And with fellow African American Suzette Charles selected as first runner-up, the 1983 pageant marked the two highest finishes ever by black contestants. A pageant official remarked: "We were very proud of [Vanessa Williams] and it encouraged other girls because it proved to them that there were no barriers. If they have what it takes, they can make it."

"I was chosen because I was qualified for the position. The fact that I was black was not a factor. I've always had to try harder in my life to achieve things, so this is regular," Vanessa commented afterward. "I don't think they chose me because . . . it's time for a black Miss America. They chose me because they thought I could do the job." Pageant chairman Marks agreed, saying that Vanessa's crowning as Miss America "should prove that you can be tops in America without regard to your color, as it should be. I can assure you that this young lady got there on her merits."

After Vanessa's win, prominent black leaders responded to the news. Congressman Charles B. Rangel of New York City said he was delighted. "It's exciting at a time when we do find separation of the races that . . . color was not a factor." Shirley Chisholm, a former Brooklyn congresswoman, agreed, "Vanessa's triumph was not trivial because it shows . . . that the country . . . seems to be trying to move toward a more egalitarian [equal] set of circumstances." And the president of the National Council of Negro Women, Dorothy Height, proclaimed, "[I]t is a very proud moment to witness . . .

it shows that once the doors are opened, people of all backgrounds feel free to enter."

Even the president of the United States wanted to congratulate the new Miss America. Vanessa received a telephone call from President Ronald Reagan at the White House, who assured her, "Your selection is not only a wonderful thing for you, it's a wonderful thing for our nation."

Nevertheless, Vanessa insisted that if any lessons were to be drawn from her capture of the Miss America crown, they were the values of hard work and education. "It shows that all things are possible. To make it for any minority or any person, you've got to have a good education. I want people to respect me . . . I'm ambitious, I have a lot of drive, and I work hard to get somewhere." Vanessa felt honored about becoming a role model for young African-American women. "By winning the title," she said, "I've shown them that black women can achieve things."

Overnight, Vanessa Williams had become a barrier breaker and a superstar. Seven years later, Miss America 1990 Debbye Turner, also African American, reflected on Vanessa's victory, saying, "When Vanessa Williams won, it caused a whole group of people to dare to dream. People who had not dared dream before for fear of being disappointed."

2

JUST A NORMAL KID
FROM MILLWOOD

— ❧ —

VANESSA LYNN WILLIAMS was born on March 18, 1963, to Helen and Milton Williams in The Bronx, New York. A year after her birth, the family moved to Millwood, New York, a predominantly white, solidly middle-class suburban town located 35 miles north of New York City.

As the first African-American family in Millwood, the Williamses were already teaching Vanessa and younger brother Chris, who was born in 1967, not to let skin color dictate what they chose to do or where they chose to live. Both parents held master's degrees in music education. Helen Williams taught singing in the Ossining, New York, public schools, and Milton taught music in the public schools of nearby Elmsford.

Vanessa's father instituted a family rule that both Vanessa and Chris study music until the age of 18. He knew that learning a musical instrument would give his children a lesson in discipline. Both children showed talent early on when they put on shows in front of their fireplace at home, singing songs from *Sesame Street*. Vanessa grew up with lessons in piano, French horn, and voice. "Music was a constant factor in our house," Vanessa recalled. "My father played all kinds of music for us—brass ensembles, show tunes, Handel's Messiah, the Temptations. Also, there was constantly the sound of my mother giving piano

Vanessa's beauty as a teenager was obvious. Her parents, however, taught her to rely on her talents and to be the best she could be in whatever she did.

lessons downstairs, my father teaching clarinet upstairs. We each had to practice a half an hour a day."

During her childhood and teenage years, Vanessa was involved in many activities. In addition to studying the French horn for nine years and the piano for five, Vanessa also played the mellophone (a brass instrument with valves that is similar in form and range to the French horn) for 14 years, took dancing, acting, and modeling lessons for six years, and performed in the school marching band.

Once Vanessa ran away into the woods that bordered her backyard in a futile effort to persuade her father to let her quit practicing her instruments. Milton persuaded her to continue, however, because he was convinced of the value of a musical education. "We were not concerned about her becoming a professional musician," Vanessa's father told an interviewer. "We wanted her to have as many options as possible. It gives her a great sense of freedom."

In addition to teaching their children the value of hard work and discipline, Helen and Milton stressed the importance of money and education. The Williamses' children had to help pay for half of any special treats, such as dress-up clothes. Although their parents often purchased the clothes in advance, the children could not wear the outfits until they earned half of the expense.

As teachers, Helen and Milton got to spend afternoons and summers with their children, and they used the time to help Vanessa and Chris study or get ahead in school. "They [my parents] used a lot of educational techniques on us," remembered Vanessa, "over dinner we had flash cards about black history."

"We never inhibited our children by telling them they couldn't do something," said Milton. "If they wanted to do a particular thing, they just had to be good at what they did."

At her parents' insistence, Vanessa began her musical education as a young child. Her talents included playing musical instruments, singing, dancing, and performing at home with her younger brother.

As Vanessa grew up, the Williamses became aware of her growing beauty, but they taught her to rely on her talents rather than her pretty face. "It was not a point in our family to focus on physical beauty," Helen said. That attitude kept Vanessa grounded, and she was never arrogant about her looks.

Although her family taught her good values, Vanessa still had a rebellious streak. At age seven, she packed her stuffed animals and ran away from home—only to return later that day. When she was 10, she defied her mother's warning about bike safety: Vanessa fell off her bike, chipped a tooth, and scarred her leg. In high school, she was punished for breaking her curfew. A neighbor, Bette Spriggs, recalled that Vanessa was an average teenager. "She was not a saint," Mrs. Spriggs said, "she was just a normal kid."

It was hard to be normal, however, when Vanessa sometimes felt different at school. She endured racial taunts but did not ask for help in confronting the problem. As her father said, "She had to live in school herself . . . we could not come there to resolve problems." While she usually felt comfortable with her classmates, Vanessa commented that "I knew I was different. I was called 'nigger.' But I never felt that an opportunity couldn't be mine because of my skin color. My mother always said, 'You're going to have to do better than anyone else just to be considered equal. But anything is possible.'" The few African-American kids in Vanessa's neighborhood all knew one another and socialized on a regular basis.

Despite the hardships of being one of the few black kids in a white community, Vanessa was a leader among her peers. Helen Williams recalls: "There was a time when girls started wearing painter's pants. It was a style in some places, but not here. Still, Vanessa thought it was a wonderful fashion statement and she started wearing them. Her friends thought it looked weird. But then . . . they were all wearing them."

Like most teenagers, Vanessa went through changes and was sometimes moody. "We saw this personality change during high school," recalled Helen. "Outside she would be cheerful and outgoing. But when she came home it was like a blue funk had swept into the house. She'd march into her room, slam the door, and not come out until dinnertime." Her father, always creative in his disciplinary tactics, decided to take Vanessa's door off its hinges. "If you are not going to communicate and be part of this family," he told her, "then you lose your privilege of privacy." It lasted one week. When her father saw a change in attitude, he put the door back up.

Throughout her years at Horace Greeley High School in the neighboring town of Chappaqua, Vanessa became a star performer. She acted in several plays and musicals. She also competed successfully for places in the All-State Woman's Choir, the All-Eastern Chorus, and the All-County Orchestra. She even traveled with the orchestra on exchange trips within the United States, visiting Miami and Boston, and

outside the country to Caracas, Venezuela, and Nassau in the Bahamas.

While still in high school, Vanessa entered her first pageant, a talent program sponsored by a fraternal group called the Masons, and finished fourth in the national competition. She was also a drama finalist in the Presidential Scholars program. Little did the talented teenager realize how both of these victories foreshadowed her future. Equally prophetic was her 1980 yearbook picture caption, which read "Follow your dream and I'll see you on Broadway."

In 1981, Vanessa's parents were proud when she enrolled at Syracuse University. Her boyfriend, Bruce Hanson, was a junior at Syracuse. The two had met at a New Year's Eve party while Vanessa was still in high school. The fact that he was white did not bother

Helen and Milton Williams instilled in their daughter the values of discipline, education, and persistence in achieving her goals. Here with her brother, Chris (left), and her parents, Vanessa appears before the media after her crowning.

Vanessa because Bruce had also grown up in an integrated environment. "He's not your average white male," Vanessa said of her first love, whom she dated for four years.

The young student began her studies in musical theater, and professors were impressed by her talent from the start. Brent Wagner, director of the musical theater program at Syracuse, told reporter Lynn Norment of *Ebony* in December 1983 that Vanessa was stylish and sophisticated, not your average college student. "She is very skilled and talented but she also has a certain degree of presence and authority that she carries onto the stage that not all beginning performers have," he said.

Vanessa found her niche in the theater department and became very popular with her classmates. A former classmate recalled a time when Vanessa was "very cool" after hearing the news that she had gotten an important part in a school production. After graciously thanking the director, however, Vanessa ran into the rehearsal room where her friends were waiting and started screaming and crying because she was so happy.

Between attending class, acting in productions, and dating Bruce, Vanessa's days were full. When the director of the local Miss Greater Syracuse Pageant saw Vanessa in a college show and approached her as a possible contestant, she was interested but felt she was simply too busy to squeeze it into her schedule. She was rehearsing for a professional production of Edmond Rostand's 1897 play *Cyrano de Bergerac* on the Syracuse campus. When *Cyrano* was canceled, however, Vanessa suddenly had more free time on her hands. She entered the pageant and won the title of Miss Greater Syracuse in April 1983.

After her victory, Vanessa never returned to college. Although she later regretted not completing college, the possibility of winning $25,000 was too great a temptation for her to not enter the Miss New York State

Pageant. At the pageant, Vanessa captivated the judges and the audience with her rendition of "Happy Days Are Here Again." In an important seven-minute interview with the judges, she deftly fielded questions about such diverse subjects as astrology, her choice of a career in music and dance, and her opinion of Chicago's first African-American mayor, Harold Washington. In addition to her dazzling talent performance and her knowledge and poise during the interview segment, Vanessa's beauty helped her become the first black woman to win the Miss New York State Pageant. The next step for Vanessa was the Miss America Pageant.

As Miss New York, Vanessa clowns with another titleholder, former World Heavyweight Champion Muhammad Ali, in Atlantic City. Wishing her well in the upcoming Miss America Pageant, Ali joked that after all his many fights, his face was still as pretty as hers.

3

AN AMERICAN TRADITION

❧

PRIOR TO HER involvement in Syracuse and New York State pageants, Vanessa had held a negative view of beauty contests. She had even referred to them as "exploitative meat shows." After competing, however, she realized that the experience would help her theatrical ambitions. Vanessa also was aware that certain reputable pageants, such as Miss America, offered incredible opportunities for young women, such as public exposure and scholarship money. She entered the Miss America preliminaries because: "[A large percentage] of the contest is based on talent. In the swimsuit competition, they want to see if you're poised and taking care of your body. And in the evening gown segment, you get a chance to make a little speech and let the audience know something about you."

As usual, Vanessa's parents were supportive of her aspirations. Helen remarked, "We didn't set out to raise a Miss America. But if our children feel qualified to do something, they should not hesitate based on someone else's prejudices."

Despite winning the local qualifiers, Vanessa conceded that as an African American, her chance of being crowned Miss America was slim. After all, the contest had officially barred minority entrants for 30 years! In 1983, minority participation in the pageant was still such a novelty that the media

Outlandish hats and lavish costumes characterized the 1923 Miss America contestants. They seemed to symbolize the high spirits of the "Roaring Twenties."

focused much of its attention on the four African-American candidates: Vanessa Williams, Suzette Charles, Deneen Graham, and Amy Elizabeth Keys. The women were asked to pose together so often that they began to joke about it. Little did any of these hopefuls realize that one of them was about to make history in the long-standing tradition of the Miss America Pageant.

In the seven decades between the first Miss America's crowning in 1921 and Vanessa Williams's appearance in 1983, the annual tradition had never lost its charm. The country's interest in this modern-day fairy tale increased each year, thanks initially to radio broadcasts from the pageant and later to movie newsreels and television coverage. The Miss American Pageant remained symbolic of what was of value in the United States through good times and bad, war and peace.

The pageant has its roots in the decade known as the "Roaring Twenties." With the end of World War I in 1918, millions of people who had sacrificed and suffered during the war years were ready to have some fun. In 1920, an amendment to the Constitution gave women the right to vote. A year earlier, another amendment had banned the manufacture or sale of alcohol, ushering in the 14-year period known as Prohibition. For the first time, people could tune their radios to hear a broadcast reporting the presidential election of Warren G. Harding. In a small resort community on the Atlantic shore in southeastern New Jersey, a group of entrepreneurs was looking for a way to extend the town's summer season past Labor Day. The group's home, Atlantic City, was known for its unique boardwalk, beautiful beaches, elegant hotels, and its steel pier, the site of odd and interesting exhibits and entertainment. Summer was a boom time for the town, but few people wanted to visit a beach resort in the fall or winter, so businesses suffered.

To boost local tourism in the fall, the Atlantic City Business Men's League decided to host a festival in September 1920. A beautiful woman dressed in flowing white robes and named "Peace" led a parade of rolling chairs, wicker hand-wheeled vehicles that are still a boardwalk feature down Atlantic Avenue.

Although the parade had been somewhat successful, in 1921 the group decided to try something different: a bathing-beauty review. They decided to call it the Atlantic City Pageant. Newspapers up and down the East Coast ran a contest urging readers to submit photos of beautiful young women. Each participating paper would select a winner and then sponsor her in

Fans line the Atlantic City Boardwalk to cheer the parading "bathing beauties" of the first pageant. In 1921, no talent competition was held, no one walked down the famous runway, and no television broadcast the event to the nation.

the pageant, where a winner would be crowned. Response was positive, especially when the idea increased newspaper sales. One newspaperman added the crowning touch to the idea when he exclaimed, "[L]et's call her 'Miss America.'"

On September 21, 1921, the first Miss America Pageant (then called the National Beauty Tournament) took place. There were eight contestants: Miss Camden, Miss Pittsburgh, Miss Ocean City, Miss Harrisburg, Miss Philadelphia, Miss Newark, Miss Atlantic City, and Miss Washington, D.C. The contestants were divided into three divisions: Professional Beauties (models and actresses), Civic Beauties, and Inter-City Beauties; all participated in the Rolling Chair Parade, Bathers' Revue, and final judging.

Miss Washington, D.C., a 16-year-old schoolgirl named Margaret Gorman, won both the judges' hearts and the first Miss America crown. Pageant officials bestowed upon their queen a replica of the Statue of Liberty's pronged tiara and a coronation robe made from a huge American flag. Margaret Gorman also received a large gold trophy showing a gilded mermaid reclining on a teakwood base which was valued at $5,000. The pageant's planners had intended that any contestant who won the Miss America title three consecutive years would be allowed to keep the trophy. No one ever managed this feat, however. By the end of the 1920s, the "Golden Mermaid," as it was called, had vanished into pageant history.

This first pageant captivated the public, generating huge amounts of publicity for Atlantic City and increasing sales for local businesses. Pleased with their plan's success, the city leaders decided to continue the event. Soon, the festival and beauty tournament achieved nationwide fame. In the years that followed, the roster of candidates swelled from eight girls to more than 70 entrants representing 36 states and Canada.

Despite its popularity, the pageant's success was interrupted by some embarrassing incidents that focused an unflattering media spotlight on the event. After officials forgot to include a no-marriage clause in the original set of rules, one first runner-up turned out to be married; another year, "Miss" Boston showed up with her husband and seven-month-old baby in tow. Another time, officials discovered that Miss Alaska was not only married but was a resident of New York City! The pageant's reputation was further tarnished when several women's clubs called the competition "indecent" and at least one New York newspaper ran a series of nasty articles. As a result of this unfavorable publicity, the National Beauty Tournament was discontinued in 1928.

The pageant was reorganized in 1935. A Chamber of Commerce civic-events coordinator from Florida became the first female pageant director. She focused her efforts on convincing the city's businessmen to try reviving the pageant and help to attract "finer types" of young ladies as contestants. Under new regulations, contestants were now required to be 18- to 28-year-old women who had never married and who would compete under the name of a city, region, or state. Contestants were prohibited from frequenting bars or nightclubs, and had a strict 1 A.M. curfew during pageant week. Hostesses, who served as chaperones, were assigned to each contestant to ensure her safety and also offer encouragement, guidance, and support. Another significant change that occurred with the pageant's return was the addition of talent as a competitive factor. By 1938, talent counted for one-third of the judges' balloting.

In September 1945, a scholarship program was unanimously sanctioned by the Board of Directors. New York's Bess Myerson became the first recipient of a Miss America scholarship. A Hunter College graduate, Myerson later used her $5,000 award for graduate studies at Columbia University. In 1946, the

The first Miss America, 16-year-old Margaret Gorman, Miss Washington, D.C., strolls down the beach at Atlantic City. Margaret was judged the winner solely on the basis of her looks.

Draped with their state banners, the 1952 Miss America contestants line up at Atlantic City Convention Hall. True to the pageant's tradition, all the participants were white.

scholarship fund totaled $25,000 and was shared by Miss America and the 15 national finalists. By the end of the 1940s, Atlantic City had become a vacation mecca again, and the Miss America Pageant was one of its biggest draws.

The golden era of the fifties was a successful decade for the pageant. Scholarship money totaled $250,000 each year, and on September 11, 1954, the Miss America Pageant was telecast live by the American Broadcasting Company (ABC). The first pageant telecast was watched by 27 million people; TV viewership tripled in the next five years.

In the 1960s, members of the women's and civil rights movements protested the Miss America Pageant. Feminists accused the pageant of degrading and exploiting women, and supporters of the civil rights movement called the pageant and its contestants "lily white." The National Association for the Advancement of Colored People (NAACP) pressed for minority participation. Despite the protests, however, the pageant remained popular and was still broadcast every year.

In 1970, Cheryl Browne became the first African American to compete in the Miss America Pageant when she won the Miss Iowa title. After her appearance in the national pageant, minority participation in the state competitions increased immediately. A decade later, in the 1980 competition, two black candidates placed in the top 10 for the first time in pageant history, and fourth runner-up, Miss Arkansas Lencola Sullivan, became the highest-placing African American ever.

Just three years later, two black candidates made it into the top five, and this time one of them, Vanessa Williams, took the crown.

4

"HERE SHE IS, MISS AMERICA!"

❦

AFTER HER WIN, Vanessa Williams became the focus of both pride and scrutiny. As Miss America, Vanessa found that she carried a double burden. She was expected to get through her year as Miss America representing the ideal woman, and she was seen as a role model and a positive example for African Americans. Remaining composed, gracious, and impeccably groomed, she spoke to black school-children about the value of education and answered tough political questions, despite the nonpartisan stance of the Miss America Pageant.

Although Vanessa came from what she described as a "deeply religious" Roman Catholic home, she claimed to be "sometimes liberal, sometimes conservative, depending on the issues." She voiced her opinion that abortion is "a right women should have"; she supported the Equal Rights Amendment (ERA), a proposed amendment to the Constitution that would prohibit discrimination on the basis of sex; and she expressed reservations about legalizing marijuana. When reporters began to ask her views on other issues, Vanessa wisely answered, "It's difficult to develop overnight opinions on things I haven't even researched."

Vanessa was the first Miss America to be interviewed at the National Press Club in Washington, D.C., and the first to attend the National Conference

Early in her tour as Miss America, Vanessa Williams is greeted by President Ronald Reagan at the White House. The President later invited Vanessa to a state dinner.

Wherever she appeared, Vanessa Williams was always gracious toward her many fans. Here, at a reception given in her honor by the National Conference of Black Mayors, Miss America signs autographs.

of Black Mayors. At the Jackie Robinson Awards dinner in New York City, she became the center of attention, unintentionally stealing the spotlight from such stars as performer Sammy Davis Jr. and tennis great Arthur Ashe. Although it was her night off, Vanessa answered questions from the press concerning the role of black women and gave her opinion about the political candidacy of the Reverend Jesse Jackson. She also signed autographs for her legion of new-found fans.

Later Vanessa told *The New York Times* reporter Susan Chira: "I didn't know I'd be scrutinized like that. I felt a lot of pressure. There were big expectations—what is she going to do to change the system? Even if there were things I was against, I could speak out against them, and it would not make the system change. Being first and different is a pleasure. But controversy gets a little strained at times."

Every Miss America's reign is extremely busy and Vanessa's was no exception. She rushed through airports and in and out of hotels with her pageant-appointed chaperone, covering 20,000 miles and visiting 200 cities, from San Juan in Puerto Rico to Anchorage, Alaska. During the long hours of travel, Vanessa usually applied her own makeup and set her hair. If she had free time, she stayed in her hotel room, ordered room service, and called her family and friends.

Vanessa traveled for a month at a time, making appearances at which she signed autographs and posed for photos. Then she took three or four days off before she was on the road again. In Cleveland, Ohio, she sang to taped music in the aisles of a department store; in Corpus Christi, Texas, she helped demonstrate corsage making at a grocery store. On a trip to Tampa, Florida, Vanessa signed autographs at a food fair sponsored by a super-market chain while surrounded by large, stuffed Cap'n Crunch, Kool-Aid, and Twinkies figures. Additionally, the pageant's four sponsors, Gillette, McDonald's, Nestlé, and American Greetings, had collectively paid a total of more than $3 million for the commercial advertise-ments that ran during the pageant. In turn, they were guaranteed at least half of Miss America's 200 appearances and could also request her company for a business lunch or dinner.

Vanessa enjoyed meeting people at her appear-ances and appointments. Some of the warmest praise came from black teenagers and their families. According to an article in *The New York Times*, at one appearance a student named Sebastien Holmes stood in line twice to meet her. The second time he greeted her, he offered Vanessa a rose. "I wanted to present this to you for all you've done for the black people, for representing us the way you've done," he said. Vanessa was touched by his compliment.

Although the pace was exhausting, Miss America was generously compensated for her time. For four hours of work, Vanessa received $1,000; if she appeared at a charitable event, the fee was $750. In addition to the $25,000 in scholarship money, Vanessa earned about $100,000 in appearance fees.

Of course, Vanessa Williams's reign was not without its glamorous moments. Her special celebrity status led to offers for Broadway shows, movies, and recording contracts—opportunities that would have to wait until her schedule became less hectic. She did, however, get the chance to perform with the Guy Lombardo Orchestra at the Waldorf Astoria Hotel in New York City on New Year's Eve and with famous vibraphonist and bandleader Lionel Hampton at a reception at the United Nations. Actor-comedian George Burns was treated to a visit by Miss America on his 80th birthday, and Vanessa fed him a piece of ceremonial birthday cake. She even accomplished another "first" for a Miss America—dining at the White House with President and Mrs. Reagan.

As Miss America, Vanessa rubbed shoulders with former Presidents Gerald Ford and Jimmy Carter, dress designers Calvin Klein and Halston, and even the cast of the television show *Happy Days*. While visiting the show's set, she met the legendary "Fonz," played by actor Henry Winkler. "It's still hard for me to think that Henry Winkler is excited to meet me and wants my autograph," Vanessa exclaimed.

Many other people too were excited to meet the new Miss America. Everywhere Vanessa went she was recognized and approached for autographs. While trying on a dress at Macy's department store in Fresno, California, a woman tried to get a glimpse of Miss America by peeping through the slats of the dressing-room door. At another time, a woman spotted Vanessa in a restaurant in Los Angeles but mistakenly asked, "Aren't you Miss Universe?" Vanessa truthfully

replied, "No," then broke into a laugh as she watched the perplexed woman walk away.

The publicity surrounding Vanessa regenerated interest in a pageant that some critics had called irrelevant and which others felt was demeaning to women. The pageant office received calls from organizations such as the Urban League, the NAACP, the United Negro College Fund, and several black universities, all wanting the young celebrity to give speeches to help raise money. Television programs that had ignored previous Miss Americas clamored for Vanessa's time, and she tried to fit in all of the requests. She made guest appearances on *The Tonight Show*, *Good Morning America*, and a Bob Hope special, and she performed a cameo role in a segment of the series *Love Boat*. One of the two pageant chaperones who accompanied

Although she did not want to be seen as a "political figure," Vanessa Williams was at ease with presidents and politicians. On Capitol Hill she chats with New York's congressman Charles Rangel (left) and senator Alphonse D'Amato.

Giving generously of her time, Vanessa often helped promote African-American causes. Flanked by Lieutenant Colonel Guion Bluford (left), the first black astronaut to travel into space, and Coretta Scott King, she speaks at a press conference during activities to honor Martin Luther King Jr.

Vanessa whenever she appeared commented, "The crowds wishing to see Miss Williams included many more blacks and people from other minority groups than before."

Although some of Vanessa's most enthusiastic supporters were African Americans, they also turned out to be her toughest critics. Some suggested the only reason she won the Miss America title was because her light skin and green eyes made her a safe choice for white America. Many African Americans did not think she was "black" enough and therefore not a good representative of black culture. "There was a lot of hype about how it wasn't a breakthrough," Vanessa said. Newspaper articles focused on her light hair color, and she received angry letters after the public learned that her boyfriend was white.

"It was like being in a political position overnight," lamented Vanessa. "People would say, 'what about black causes?' . . . I would say 'I'm only 20 years old. What qualifies me to answer?'"

Months into her reign, Vanessa hoped the publicity surrounding her would focus less on skin color and more on her career aspirations. Instead of asking her questions about her acting or singing, however, the press continued to hound her about racial and political issues. Frustrated, Vanessa attempted to remove herself from the cameras. At her speaking appearances, she continued to talk about the importance of education and the desire to succeed. When she walked on stage in a high school in Atlanta, Georgia, a group of 4,000 African-American students begged her to sing. She was delighted to perform and not be subjected to the usual onslaught of reporters' questions.

Throughout her reign, Vanessa maintained her composure despite intense public scrutiny. As her term neared an end, she reflected: "The first few months were really hard, handling being a celebrity, a role model, what was expected of me, the controversy, the media. I hardly got any sleep, I was sick after the first weekend." After those months she said she understood what the pageant's panel of judges was looking for when they chose a winner. "It's not the person who's got the best talent, not the best looking, not even the most intelligent," Vanessa said, "it's the person who is the most well-balanced mentally, the one who has the guts and the endurance to make it through the year."

Unfortunately, Vanessa never made it through her year as Miss America. It was not due to a lack of stamina, however. In July 1984, 10 months into her one-year reign, a scandal broke like an unexpected summer storm.

5

THE FALL

ON FRIDAY, JULY 13, 1984, Vanessa received
an anonymous phone call. The caller informed her
that photographs depicting her nude were going to
appear in the September issue of *Penthouse*. At first
she thought it was a prank, but she soon remembered
the pictures to which the person was referring.

In June 1982, after her freshman year at Syracuse,
Vanessa had taken a summer job as a receptionist and
makeup artist for Tom Chiapel, photographer and
co-owner of a local model registry in Mt. Kisco, New
York. "Tom had expressed an interest in nude photog-
raphy and asked me if I'd [model nude]," Vanessa
recalled. "I had never done it before. I was a bit curious,
but I didn't know if I wanted to take the chance." She
finally agreed to a photo session with Chiapel but only
after he assured her that they would be the only ones to
see the photos.

"I'm still not sure exactly why I did it," Vanessa
explained when she was asked why she had posed
for Chiapel. "I was young. I was curious . . . I was
feeling like my own woman—free, rebellious, my
own person. I didn't want to do anything conven-
tional for a summer job, and I was really getting
into the whole models-photographer's world."

Later that summer, Chiapel asked Vanessa to pose
nude with another female model in silhouette. The
pictures would not show the models' faces but would

instead focus on the outlines of their bodies. He told her that both models would be unidentifiable. "He [Chiapel] assured me nothing would happen and I trusted him," Vanessa said. Chiapel broke that trust just a year later, after Vanessa was crowned Miss America. Eager to cash in on the success of one of his former models, Chiapel sold the photos to *Penthouse* editor and publisher Bob Guccione.

When she learned about the photos, Vanessa wanted to inform pageant officials before the magazine was distributed. She called pageant chairman Albert Marks Jr. "We've been through lots of things, we all make mistakes," he reassured her. "I thought he would believe in me enough as a Miss America to hear my side, especially after I confided in them," Vanessa said of the incident. "I told them because, in case the rumors were true, I wanted to save them embarrassment."

Although Vanessa had been up front with the pageant officials about the situation, they were not as straightforward with her. Through her lawyer, she learned that the pageant had issued a press release on July 20 giving her 72 hours to resign. Pageant officials cited two sections of the agreement signed by each national finalist that made their case for Vanessa's resignation. One dealt with morals and the pageant's image, requiring contestants to certify that they had not been involved in any acts that the pageant considered "immoral." The officials did not specify their definition of immorality, however. The other section mentioned a need to "uphold" the contest's image.

During the weekend after the pageant's request for her resignation, Vanessa met with lawyers and her family in seclusion in New York City. On Monday, July 23, 1984, an emotionally drained Vanessa Williams announced she would step down as Miss America. "It is apparent to me now that because of all that has happened during the past week, it would be difficult to make appearances as Miss America," she

said at a crowded press conference at the Sheraton Centre Hotel in Manhattan. She went on to say that she wished she could retain her title but mentioned "potential harm to the pageant and the deep, deep division that a bitter fight may cause" as reasons that she could not.

"I'm not stupid and I know those pictures are very incriminating," Vanessa told a reporter from *The New York Times* after the press conference. "They indicate a life style that is not mine. It is important for me, for my peace of mind, to say that I am not like that. They were just a few hours of my life."

In stepping down, Vanessa became the only winner ever to abdicate the Miss America throne. First runner-up Suzette Charles stepped in for the remaining seven weeks of Vanessa's reign. Vanessa was allowed to keep the money she had earned in personal appearances

Waving the cover of the Penthouse *issue that displayed Vanessa's nude photos, pageant official Albert Marks Jr. appears at a press conference and announces that pageant officials had no choice but to ask Vanessa to relinquish her crown.*

fees while she held the title as well as the $25,000 college scholarship, but this compensation could not heal her broken heart or bruised ego.

To further Vanessa's humiliation, the day before her resignation, the September 1984 edition of *Penthouse* hit newsstands. That issue, marking the 15th anniversary of the magazine, combined with the November issue (in which Vanessa's photos reappeared) to sell 10 million copies and gross *Penthouse* some $37 million in sales. Guccione, who confessed that the magazine had not attempted to get Vanessa's permission before publishing the photographs, did say he was sorry that she had resigned. He did not, however, express any guilt on his part. "I don't feel that I'm responsible for it," he commented, "my obligation was to my readers. This was an interesting bit of highly newsworthy information and photographs." Guccione further confided to a *People* reporter, "It's made her by far the most famous Miss America that ever lived."

While Guccione may have thought the photos would help Vanessa's career in the long run, she was devastated by their immediate impact. She later described the time between the anonymous call and the press conference as "the worst week of my life, the worst thing that ever happened to me," and said that she felt "violated" by both *Penthouse* and by the officials of the Miss America Pageant. Vanessa's vulnerability prompted feminists such as Gloria Steinem and Susan Brownmiller and black leaders such as Jesse Jackson and Benjamin Hooks to rally to her defense. In addition, friends and strangers sent flowers to the Williams' home and called to offer encouragement and support. The only people who never contacted Vanessa were the Miss America officials. "I felt it was a lack of sensitivity on the part of the officials," Helen Williams said. "It disturbed me that they did not have the courage to say to us: 'We made this decision. It's something we have to do.' Not a word. Nothing."

Cameras and reporters arrived at the house with the brass doorplate that read "Home of Miss America," but Vanessa was not there. "She's away from here in a secure place, where she can rest," Vanessa's father told the media. "She was shocked when she heard the news and she became depressed. But we were able to see her briefly last night, and we gave her a good hug."

Vanessa's parents were supportive throughout the ordeal. As Helen explained, "[M]any young people I know, even myself when I was younger, do things on a whim and they later think their parents will kill them if they ever found out." She claimed that members of the family did not try to hide from the media or other prying eyes. They answered the door, picked up the phone, and sat on the living room couch with the drapes open. "We believe in being honest with the world," Helen said. "That's something we've taught our children and we intend to stay that way."

Vanessa eventually returned home, but it was not to the peace and quiet she had known before the scandal. As strangers hurled insults from passing cars, she winced and fought back the urge to cry. She was humiliated when a comedian made jokes at her expense on a television show. "It hurts a lot," Vanessa said. "My mother goes to the supermarket and hears people talking about it, and kids in cars scream awful things when they pass the house. But I try not to see them. I focus in on the people who still call the house and ask, 'How's Vanessa doing?' and the people who write me letters and stop me on the street and say, 'We still love you.'"

Despite the scandal, Millwood's pride in Vanessa Williams remained intact. A tree in the center of town boasted a hand-painted sign that read: "Millwood N.Y. ❤ Vanessa with or without her crown." Lloyd S. Howard, a Millwood resident of 30 years, remarked, "Vanessa is a highly articulate, bright young lady who did something when she was

JUDGE NOT THAT YE BE NOT JUDGED

WE SUPPORT AND LOVE YOU

SISTER AMERICA

Vanessa We Love you And We Always will Love And RESPECT you!!!!...

LONG LIVE THE QUEEN SUPPORT VANES BOYCOTT

Vanessa was not without support as well-wishers and friends sent flowers and cards to Vanessa's home in Millwood. Others, like these demonstrators, marched and carried signs protesting the pageant's decision to recall her title.

younger and now someone is trying to exploit her with it."

Vanessa's few hours of curiosity in posing nude had a profound impact on her life. The scandal brought an abrupt end to traveling. It also canceled the lucrative personal appearances and endorsement deals that she had hoped would pay for her acting career, including a six-figure, nine-year contract with the Gillette Company. She and Bruce also ended their four-year relationship, although Vanessa claimed the controversy was not the reason.

Vanessa now spent her time in the company of lawyers and advisers, trying to decide how her future would be affected. One of her most comforting new professional relationships was with Ramon Hervey, a public relations expert from Los Angeles who had been hired to coach Vanessa on her resignation speech and combat the negative press surrounding the release of the photos. He also helped Vanessa sort through the many questions she had concerning her future: Should she return to school? Pursue a role in a movie? Hope for a part in a Broadway show?

To keep her mind off the scandal, Vanessa began auditioning for new parts. Prior to her resignation, she had been offered roles in several new projects and had also completed a guest appearance on a new television series, *Partners in Crime*, starring Linda Carter and Loni Anderson. Following the scandal, however, Vanessa suffered several rejections. She tried out for the part of Musetta in Joseph Papp's production of Puccini's famous opera *La Boheme*. But the role calls for a soprano, a voice that reaches the highest ranges, and Vanessa has a lower-range alto voice. She also talked with Tommy Tune about playing the lead in the Gershwin musical *My One and Only* when former model Twiggy left the role. Lee Gershwin, wife of the show's lyricist Ira Gershwin, nixed the idea, fearing Vanessa Williams would attract the wrong sort of audience. Vanessa was also passed over for a musical version of the horror flick *Carrie*, after the director and producer decided they did not want to use a black actress for the role.

Vanessa wanted to work, not only for the distraction it offered and for her love of performing but also because her money was running out. "I know everybody thinks, 'Oh she has it made,'" Vanessa said. "But they don't realize that I was Miss America for less than one year. Most of the money I saved is going to pay lawyers' fees."

Vanessa filed a lawsuit against Guccione and Chiapel, contending she never signed a model's release for Chiapel. Guccione, however, claimed that

Resisting the temptation to drop out of sight, Vanessa began getting her life back in order. Pursuing her dream of appearing in a Broadway show, she began rehearsals for a new musical, One Man Band, *to open in June 1985.*

she had signed a release, and the suit was eventually dropped. "I guess no one owns the right to the pictures. It's a legal question," Vanessa said. "I don't recall signing anything with Tom Chiapel. I remember signing a stat[istic] sheet as a model. Every model at the registry had to fill one out."

In addition to her money woes, Vanessa was constantly reminded of the approaching 1984 Miss America Pageant. The dress she was supposed to have worn for her final promenade down the runway as Miss America had already been ordered—a flowing white lace gown with little seed pearls. Instead of participating, she watched the pageant on television. It reminded her of the times when she was a little girl, happy to stay up late so that she could see the women in their pretty evening gowns. Even then, she never dreamed of becoming Miss America. "It was a lovely fantasy," she said after her resignation. "I worked so hard. I'm sure I'll be very emotional when I watch it. I'm really curious how it looks now from this side. I may not have wanted to be a beauty queen all my life. But I didn't want things this way."

At the time of Vanessa's resignation, pageant officials said there would be no mention of her reign other than listing her name with other former winners, noting that she had resigned. Later, however, they had a change of heart. The brochure for the September 15, 1984, pageant included two pages dedicated to Vanessa.

Twenty-one-year-old Vanessa Williams now had two choices: she could drop out of sight, or she could forge ahead with her career, hoping that her true talent would eventually overshadow her youthful indiscretion. She chose the latter, more difficult path.

6

PICKING UP THE PIECES

❦

Furthering her career as a singing star, Vanessa records the song "Love Is," the main theme for a new soundtrack to the television series Beverly Hills 90210. *Her superb voice and good looks made her a natural for a musical career.*

AFTER THE *PENTHOUSE* scandal, people predicted that Vanessa Williams's career was over before it had even begun. As frightened as she was about her future, however, Vanessa never stopped believing that she would one day prove them wrong. Still, Vanessa was concerned about the scandal's effect on her family. As it turned out, however, her parents and brother were her greatest source of strength. "I became flooded with fear," Vanessa said of her reaction to the photos, "more for what my parents might think and for any pain I might have caused them than for myself. But when I told them the facts and that I was sorry, they simply said, 'You're our daughter. We love you.'"

With her parents' support, Vanessa felt her own strength return. "That was the key to my surviving, to picking myself up and getting on with it," she commented later. Vanessa also had others rooting for her. Ramon Hervey, who had become her official publicist during the scandal, was a trusted friend. "You're young, you'll get over this," he assured her. Besides a good working relationship, the two also developed a close personal bond. "I instantly found his calm and sense of security reassuring and appealing," Vanessa recalled.

Vanessa was eager for Hervey to become her personal manager. As a partner in a public relations firm known as The Group, Hervey had handled publicity for a variety of celebrities including superstars Natalie Cole, Richard Pryor, and Bette Midler. Although at first reluctant to represent Vanessa, Hervey soon recognized her talent and wanted to help her succeed. It would take some work to convince the decision makers in the entertainment industry that Vanessa could be a star, however. As Miss America, "She had notoriety and . . . celebrity, but she really didn't have a lot of acting credibility," Hervey explained.

To acquire some acting experience, he advised Vanessa to seek out television roles. What followed were guest spots in several forgettable network series such as *Partners in Crime* (1984) and a sitcom called *He's the Mayor* (1986). Public reaction to Vanessa on camera was mixed. Many people saw her as a "scandal-ridden beauty queen" who suddenly thought she could act, instead of someone who had been training for years before the *Penthouse* incident.

Marketing Vanessa was difficult for Hervey. Although she regularly received scripts, most of them were exploitative vehicles attempting to capitalize on her name. "I've gotten lots of things with titles like *Satan and Eve*," Vanessa said. "You know things that begin 'their oiled bodies clashed in the mud,' really ridiculous stuff." Against Hervey's advice, Vanessa did eventually star in the 1989 television movie *Full Exposure: The Sex Tapes Scandal*, in which the story line closely resembled her own troubles with the *Penthouse* pictures.

Vanessa did manage to land small roles in the feature films *The Pick Up Artist* and *Under the Gun*, but she craved more steady work. "The problem is that Vanessa has these two images: one represented by the symbol of Miss America, the other by those pictures," Hervey said. "Well, neither one of those images is totally representative of who Vanessa Williams is as a person."

In 1986, Hervey came up with another idea. He introduced Vanessa to his good friend Ed Eckstine, who was starting up a new label at PolyGram Records. Hervey knew that with her good looks and beautiful singing voice, Vanessa could break into the music business. Although Eckstine had heard Vanessa sing during the pageant, he was even more impressed in person. "But she was raised in New York listening to black radio," Eckstine later commented. "She knew everything from seminal hip hop to Angela Bofill, to funk, to the stuff Shep Pettibone used to play." Eckstine signed Vanessa to his new label, Wing, a division of PolyGram.

While the record deal was being cemented, the relationship between Hervey and Vanessa grew more intense, and they fell in love. Vanessa described her feelings: "I now believe Ramon's coming into my life . . . was God's way of saying, 'Out of tremendous tragedy, some light will be shone on you.'" In January 1987, 35-year-old Ramon Hervey and 24-year-old Vanessa Williams were married. They bought an apartment in Laderas Heights, California, a suburb of Los Angeles, and were soon in the recording studio, tending to Vanessa's budding career.

The product of their efforts was her debut album, *The Right Stuff*, released in 1988. "When it finally came to putting together *The Right Stuff* . . . we didn't want to be disposably dancey or 'Here She Is Miss America'—the exploitation of all that," Eckstine said. "We virtually had no songs given to us," Vanessa recalled. "So we had to beg, borrow, and steal to get any kind of material." Although she had always believed that she would make her mark in the field of acting, Vanessa soon found herself a recording star.

The Right Stuff made an immediate impact on the pop and R&B (Rhythm-and-Blues) charts with four hits: "Dreamin," "Darling I," "He's Got the Look," and the title track, a dance/pop/R&B smash. The hit singles and videos the album spawned earned Vanessa

Vanessa Williams has said that Ramon Hervey, here with a beaming Vanessa on their wedding day, was her "knight in shining armor," the one who became her rescuer and protector after the devastating scandal.

three Grammy nominations and the NAACP's Best New Artist Award. One reviewer wrote, "The disc has a consistent feel. . . . [Vanessa is] smart enough to . . . let her personality take up the slack." *The Right Stuff* was embraced by radio listeners and went gold, with more than 600,000 copies sold.

Although she wanted both a family and a successful career, Vanessa learned to curb her anxiety. "It'll all happen," she told *Ebony* reporter Charles Whitaker of the life she sought. "I'm only 24. I can't be greedy. I'm just going to work on my career and enjoy my life. I don't want to become so obsessed that I miss out on the other things life has to offer."

One of those things was children. In 1988, a daughter named Melanie was born. She was followed by a second daughter, Jillian, in 1990. Vanessa and Ramon were thrilled to be parents. But Vanessa proved to Ed Eckstine that being a mother would not interfere with her recording career. "The next phase is making sure you are taken seriously as a recording artist," Vanessa said of her career responsibilities. "You have to prove that you are in it for the long haul. . . . The new [album] will be a much stronger record, just because I'll be much more confident."

Before the release of her next album, Vanessa began hosting *The Soul of VH-1*, a weekly one-hour R&B tribute featuring new videos and classic clips of older songs, on the music cable channel VH-1. "We chose Vanessa because of her talents as a recording artist," explained a VH-1 executive. "She understands the music she's talking about and she contributes that knowledge to the scripts." At 28, Vanessa was becoming a significant presence in the entertainment world. She also found that the more work she did, the less talk there was of her lost Miss America crown.

To give thanks for her success and happiness, Vanessa decided to give back to the community by doing charity work. In 1989, she took part in an East

Coast radio station's Coats for Kids campaign. She also contributed her rendition of the song "What Child Is This?" to the album *A Very Special Christmas 2*. Proceeds from album sales benefited the Special Olympics. In addition to her recording and charity work, Vanessa starred in a number of televised special events. They included the Emmy Award-winning *Motown Returns to the Apollo*, Eddie Murphy Production's *The Boy Who Loved Christmas*, the CBS-TV movie *Stompin' at the Savoy*, and a Perry Mason movie of the week entitled *The Case of the Silenced Singer*.

With so much to keep her busy, time passed quickly for Vanessa. In 1991 she released her new album, *The Comfort Zone*. Eckstine described it as "a dancey vibe, a jazz vibe, a ballady vibe." Vanessa's new vocal style was soulful and seductive, reminiscent of a 1940s' lounge singer. The first single, "Runnin' Back to You," hit number 1 on the R&B and dance charts. But it was the unforgettable "Save the Best for Last" that captivated audiences, topped the pop charts for six weeks, and finally convinced Vanessa that she was a star. "I think that was the first time when I felt, finally, I'm on my way," she told *Harper's Bazaar*. She even got the opportunity to sing the ballad at President Bill Clinton's inaugural festivities in 1993. Music critic Alex Henderson noted that "Vanessa Williams is at her most exciting when taking chances and coming from the heart." *The Comfort Zone* was nominated for a Grammy Award and went platinum, selling more than one million copies.

Even though her music career was thriving, Vanessa decided to continue acting. She appeared with Richard Pryor and Gene Wilder in *Another You*, as Pryor's love interest. She also sang a couple of songs as Lulu in the futuristic film *Harley Davidson and the Marlboro Man* with Mickey Rourke and Don Johnson. Although neither film was a box-office success, Vanessa enjoyed the experience and the exposure as a serious actress.

With her list of on-screen credits growing, Vanessa decided to join the Screen Actor's Guild (SAG), an organization to which most film actors belong. SAG is a trade union that promotes safe working conditions and rights for its members, in addition to hosting the occasional fancy party or Hollywood function. It is considered a sign of prestige if an actor belongs to the organization because he or she must have proof of having acted in a professional job before joining. Unfortunately, another actress was already registered under the name Vanessa Williams, so Vanessa added her middle initial and became Vanessa L. Williams. Although Vanessa's middle initial appears on all of her film credits, her name remains simply Vanessa Williams on her album covers (her recording career is not regulated by SAG).

Playing a singer at a rock 'n roll bar, Vanessa got the chance to act as well as sing in the futuristic Western film Harley Davidson and the Marlboro Man *with Mickey Rourke (center) and Don Johnson.*

Vanessa took some much-needed time off in 1993 when she gave birth to a boy named Devin, expanding the family to five. Despite some marital problems and subsequent marriage counseling, Vanessa was content in her roles as mother, music artist, and actress. Less than a year after the birth of her son, Vanessa was at work on her third album—*The Sweetest Days*. More diverse than Vanessa's two previous albums, it included 12 songs, among them "Long Way Home," "Constantly," "Moonlight over Paris," "Sister Moon" (written by Sting), and "Ellamental." The last was a unique R&B/jazz/hip-hop tribute to Ella Fitzgerald and was recorded with legendary musicians Toots Theilman on harmonica and Roy Hargrove playing trumpet solos. "That whole Ella era of jazz and women in jazz was a very respectable and classy time to be an entertainer," said Vanessa of her tribute.

The first single to be released off the album was the title track, "The Sweetest Days," a ballad inspired by a conversation Vanessa had with writer Phil Gardston about marriage, children, and relationships. The theme of the song is about relishing the moment and appreciating the time with family and friends. In addition, "Love Is," a top-10 hit duet with Brian McKnight, was featured on the soundtrack of the popular television show *Beverly Hills 90210*. In order to achieve the proper laid-back mood to the music, Vanessa and her guitarist worked with lava lamps glowing, incense burning, and candles flickering.

In the spring of 1994, as Vanessa's third album was about to take the music charts by storm, Canadian producer Garth Drabinsky was searching for a lead to temporarily replace Chita Rivera in Broadway's *Kiss of the Spider Woman*. When Vanessa traveled to Toronto to audition for the lead in the revival of the musical *Showboat*, Drabinsky, who was involved in casting for both *Showboat* and *Kiss of the Spider Woman*, knew that he had found his replacement

Backstage at Broadway's Broadhurst Theater, Vanessa talks about her starring role in The Kiss of the Spider Woman. *Her career skyrocketed when she got rave reviews for her performance.*

for Rivera. He offered Vanessa the title role in a limited summer run. The family moved back to the East Coast and settled into a house in Westchester County, New York, just 10 minutes from the place where Vanessa had grown up.

Preparing for Broadway was hard work, even for someone as disciplined as Vanessa. The cast was plagued with bad luck before the show even opened. Just a week before the big night, Vanessa gashed her knee open and it swelled up. Fortunately, she did not limp onstage. In addition, one of the two male stars tore a vocal chord, and the other was hit by a car while riding his bike on the day of the opening. For the first weeks Vanessa worked with understudies.

Despite all of these catastrophes, nothing could diminish the excitement of the evening of June 27, 1994, when Vanessa's Broadway dream was realized. Dressed in top hat, tails, and flashing a big grin, Vanessa never let the audience know how nervous she felt. Her part in this intriguing drama was demanding, as she had to play two women rolled into one. The story tells of two men—one a Marxist revolutionary, the other a gay window-dresser—sharing a cell in a South American prison. "They escape the atrocities of this day-to-day gruesome life by escaping to a fantasy world of a woman named Aurora, who was a movie star in the 1940s. So my role is a dual role between Aurora and the Spider Woman," Vanessa told *Jet*.

Critical reaction to her performance was enthusiastic. "When she sings, her voice fills the theater, ringing with tender sympathy or booming with sexy menace," Vincent Canby wrote for *The New York Times*. "Her stage manner is both playful and aloof. She's not a performer who holds back. She's throwing everything she has into this performance. In the way the role worked for the incomparable Chita Rivera, Aurora [the Spider Woman] is now rewarding the gorgeous Vanessa Williams." Vanessa's performance also boosted ticket sales by as much as $100,000 a week. "She has her own following," Drabinsky noted. "Obviously, she's appealing to a younger audience than Chita did and to a black audience." Vanessa was so successful in the role that her contract was extended.

Backstage after a performance, Williams was often visited by reporters. Her dressing room, crowded with floral tributes, all hung upside down to dry, was also filled with brightly colored greeting cards, including one from her kids that read "Good Luck Spider Mommy." Still, she admitted she had been terrified at the thought of following Rivera, a musical-theater legend, in the role of Aurora. "I was probably a little nervous," Vanessa confided to an interviewer about her audition for *Kiss of the Spider Woman* with director Harold Prince and composer John Kander. Her fears were soon replaced with happiness and confidence, however, as her eight-month Broadway stint was a hit. "I finally got a chance to show people my forte—musical theater," said Vanessa. "This was a dream come true for me."

As an all-around performer, Vanessa felt she had finally arrived. She was now living the life she had always dreamed for herself. "I think I found my direction, which is to go in many directions," she said after the opening. She harked back to the golden days of movie musicals when actors were often "triple threats: you sang, you danced, you acted." Some 10 years after the scandal, Vanessa felt she had the courage to face any obstacle and the talent to make further dreams come true.

7

A TRIPLE THREAT

A S SOON AS Vanessa's Broadway run ended in February 1995, producer Robert Halmi approached her to star in the ABC-TV remake of another successful Broadway musical, *Bye Bye Birdie*. Vanessa accepted the chance to portray Rose, the girlfriend of a songwriter named Albert (played by Jason Alexander of television's *Seinfeld*). The plot revolved around two themes: Albert and his attempt to write a hit song for teen idol Conrad Birdie, and Rose and her desire to marry Albert after their lengthy courtship. The role gave Vanessa the chance to sing five songs, act, and show off her dancing skills.

She also found the time to record the song "Colors of the Wind" for the Walt Disney animated feature film *Pocahontas*. The song became a top-40 hit and won the Academy Award for Best Song in 1996. Even more importantly, the song made Vanessa a star to her children, who loved Disney movies. The entire family was treated to a trip to Disney World, where they were given the royal treatment. The Herveys also traveled together to the Super Bowl in January 1996, where Vanessa belted out the national anthem to a packed stadium.

In 1995, Ramon Hervey had learned that producers were looking for a female lead for Arnold Schwarzenegger's film *Eraser*. Eager for the chance to

By the time Vanessa performed the song "Colors of the Wind" at the 1996 Academy Awards in Los Angeles, she was a top recording star and an established film and television personality.

star in a potential blockbuster, Vanessa booked a flight to Los Angeles for a meeting with the film's director and producer. A few days later, they flew her back for a screen test with Schwarzenegger.

Landing the role in *Eraser* was no easy task. Although Vanessa had enjoyed success in the music industry and on Broadway, the producers were not certain that she had the ability to handle the pressure of a big-budget motion picture. When Schwarzenegger's wife, television reporter Maria Shriver, saw a tape of Vanessa's screen test, however, she campaigned for Vanessa to get the part. Shriver's efforts paid off when Vanessa was offered the role.

Not only did Vanessa land her first big movie role she also forged a new friendship with Maria and Arnold. Vanessa admitted at first to being "intimidated by [Arnold's] presence," but the Schwarzeneggers quickly put her at ease. Maria invited Vanessa to their home for dinner, and Arnold pointed out the similarities in their careers. He had begun as a body-builder who had won the Mr. Universe title five times. Arnold's chances of film stardom had seemed very dim, but he had proven the skeptics wrong by going on to become one of the biggest names in the film world.

Vanessa had also become famous for her good looks but was showing the public that her talent exceeded her beauty. "My role is great because there are a couple of nice acting pieces," Vanessa told a *Sacramento Bee* reporter. Portraying Lee Cullen, a woman in the federal government's witness protection program who is forced to change her identity after testifying, Vanessa jumped off gangplanks and fought atop speeding trains. Luckily, having just come off her Broadway run and the filming of *Bye Bye Birdie,* Vanessa was in great physical shape. In addition to working out with a trainer two hours a day, she cut out dairy products and caffeine and went on a personalized nutrition program for extra stamina during her scenes. Proving her versatility, between

takes Vanessa recorded the song "Where Do We Go from Here" for the film's soundtrack.

During filming, Vanessa was treated to visits from Ramon and the kids. Her six-year-old daughter Jillian showed that like her mother, she too was artistic and enterprising. Jillian sold her drawings to people on the set. She even made a sketch of Arnold and then sold it to him for a quarter.

When the film opened, Vanessa earned praise from the Schwarzeneggers as well as the fans who helped the film gross more than $100 million. "You showed them that you have guts. I like strong women," Arnold told Vanessa. Rounding out Vanessa's

Vanessa Williams and Arnold Schwarzenegger confer with director Charles Russell on the set of the action-thriller Eraser. *Arnold admired Vanessa's courage and ambition and complimented her by saying how much he admired strong women.*

success in 1996 was the release of her fourth album, *Star Bright,* a collection of holiday and Christmas songs. Critic Rodney Batdorf called it "pleasant background music" and went on to say that Vanessa has "an engaging voice . . . the music is familiar, making it a nice seasonal album."

While Vanessa's career showed no signs of slowing down, her marriage was deteriorating. "We started marriage counseling in 1989 or 1990. The dynamics changed as I got bigger and bigger and made money," Vanessa admitted. Friends of the couple claimed that Ramon was not faithful to his wife and that Vanessa had had enough. "It's one thing to forgive once, but when a pattern of behavior that is dangerous for my health, embarrassing and humiliating for me and my family . . . it's intolerable," said Vanessa.

She had stayed in the marriage because she wanted it to work and she was grateful to Hervey for his help with her career. Nevertheless, Vanessa claimed that her success was of her own making. "We certainly worked as a team," she said of the early years of their marriage. "But he [Hervey] did not create a singer. He did not teach me how to sing, how to dance, how to act. We worked very hard together as a team to make sure that the choices for my career would happen." She remarked that even without Hervey "I would have gone through the same amount of press scrutiny, but once the dust settles, it doesn't negate your talent, and it didn't take away my fire and desire to prove and to work."

Vanessa shared the blame for the failure of the marriage, however. "Maybe I spent too much time with my kids. Maybe I didn't spend enough time with my husband or make him my first priority. . . . Marriage is a partnership and it does take some give-and-take, but it also takes constant support and understanding and communication." After a two-year separation, the couple divorced in 1997.

Suddenly, Vanessa was a single mom, and the

stress was intense. She developed an eating disorder because of the pressures of work and home. "I'd get on the treadmill and do an hour. My stomach was too tense," she said of the time following her divorce. "When I get nervous, I can't eat. People kept telling me how great I looked. But your clothes are falling off, and you can't face another day. So I was looking my best when I was the most miserable." She got healthy again when she realized that her three children needed her even more than before the divorce.

Vanessa chose to stay in Westchester County, near her parents and her childhood home because she wanted her children to have a normal life, something that she felt was not possible in Hollywood. Ramon also remained in the area to be close to his children. Vanessa, Melanie, Jillian, and Devin lived in temporary quarters while a turn-of-the-century fieldstone farmhouse Vanessa had purchased was being rebuilt into the family's dream home. Once completed, the house included a deluxe master bedroom as well as bedrooms for each of the children, a study, a workout room, a swimming pool, and a Jacuzzi. The grounds, which were once a pasture, contained a huge, sloping front lawn with a pond. Joining the family in their new hilltop home were Sebastian, their Shih Tzu dog, and two turtles. Live-in nanny, Kathianne Mead, was also an important part of life in the Williams home.

The girls took music lessons from Vanessa's parents as well as dance lessons from the same instructors who had tutored Vanessa as a child. All of the children got to see their father regularly, and Ramon and Vanessa maintained an amicable relationship. "It'll never be one of those relationships where when one of the kids get married it's 'Oh my God! Mom and Dad sitting in the same pew!'" Vanessa explained.

Vanessa's confidence as a mother increased after the divorce. She knew that she had to be physically and mentally balanced in order to juggle the demands of her career and of her children. Still, she made certain that the children were always her top priority. "If my career was too stressful . . . I could definitely give it up. . . . I have my responsibilities. I brought these kids into the world, and now I have to do the best job I can."

Despite her familial responsibilities, Vanessa managed to keep working at an incredible pace. Besides the care given to her kids by Kathianne, Vanessa's parents were always willing to watch their grandchildren. This freedom allowed Vanessa to travel to Turkey to shoot NBC's made-for-television miniseries *The Odyssey*, based on the Greek epic by Homer. Vanessa played the seductive goddess Calypso, who offers Odysseus immortality if he will end his quest to return to his home and wife in Ithaca. The all-star cast also included Armand Assante, Isabella Rossellini, and Bernadette Peters. While on location, Vanessa met the production's screenwriter, Christopher Solimine. Although the two were in the same class at Syracuse University, they had never met. They soon began dating.

Next up for Vanessa was the MGM/United Artists Pictures film *Hoodlum*, in which she played Francine Hughes, a woman who falls in love with a gangster played by Laurence Fishburne. "Most of our scenes were very intense and emotional. It was critical that we establish a relationship," Vanessa said of her costar. The film was set in the 1930s, and Vanessa had fun dressing for the role as well as acting in a period piece. The film did well at the box office despite less-than-stellar reviews for the actors. The one exception to the critics' negative comments was Vanessa. *Los Angeles Times* film critic Kenneth Turan wrote, "Williams does all she's asked to do in this largely window dressing role, which is more than some of the rest of the cast can manage."

Much better received by critics was the 1997 release *Soul Food*. This surprise hit film was a family

Vanessa enjoyed her role as Calypso, the seductive enchantress in the television miniseries The Odyssey. *She noted that the producers ". . . wrote the role for me, which is nice, to have ancient history rewritten just for you."*

Furthering her film career, and receiving accolades for her role, Vanessa (center) appeared as one of three sisters, along with Vivica A. Fox (left) and Nia Long in the box office hit Soul Food.

drama about three sisters who meet at their mother's house every week for Sunday night dinner. Vanessa garnered raves for her work as Teri, the uptight older sister of the family. A *Los Angeles Times* film critic praised Vanessa as possessing "fierce intelligence and honesty" in the role. Although it cost only $7.5 million to make, *Soul Food* grossed an impressive $114 million.

Vanessa's fifth album, *Next*, was released in midsummer 1997. Critic Leo Stanley wrote in the annual *All Music Guide* that Williams "has grown into a strong singer, capable of wringing emotion out of even banal adult contemporary tracks . . . when she has a good song, like the sultry 'Someone Like You' the results are first-rate. . . . [*Next* is] a worthwhile effort from Williams." Following the album's release,

Vanessa took off on a successful six-week concert tour across the United States with her friend, Grammy Award winning R&B vocalist Luther Vandross.

Professionally, 1997 was an incredibly busy and successful year for Vanessa. Now considered an actress, singer, and dancer, with an impressive list of film, television, and recording credits by anyone's standards, she was not content to rest on her past achievements. Vanessa entered the new year with more new projects on her horizon.

8

"SAVE THE BEST FOR LAST"

❧

"**M**OVIES ARE GREAT, but for me Broadway is the ultimate," Vanessa confided after her run in *Kiss of the Spider Woman*. "I get to sing, dance, act, and work with an ensemble cast every night. I can come home at night and wake up with my kids in the morning. I can't wait to get back."

Vanessa got the chance to return to the New York stage in 1998's revival of *St. Louis Woman* at the City Center. As in *Kiss of the Spider Woman*, she played the title role, Della Green, the object of many men's desire. Originally produced for the stage in 1946, *St. Louis Woman* tells the story of a late 19th-century black saloon society built around horse racing.

Although the revival, part of a series called "Encores: Great American Musicals in Concert" was a limited engagement, Vanessa was praised for her portrayal of Della. *The New York Times* theater critic Ben Brantley wrote that she "gives a smooth, lustrous performance, wearing her preternatural beauty without self-consciousness and bringing a polished professionalism to every note and line."

Vanessa wished the run could have been extended, but she had other projects awaiting her attention. She costarred with Latin pop star Chayanne in *Dance with Me*, a movie that portrays the world of competitive Latin ballroom dancing. Vanessa's character, Ruby, is a heartbroken dance instructor and single

Flashing a broad smile, Vanessa poses with the Image Award she won as Outstanding Actress in a Motion Picture for her role in Soul Food. The Image Awards, given by the NAACP, pay tribute to persons who work for positive change for blacks in the entertainment industry.

Vanessa enjoys a moment together with her daughter, Melanie. A devoted mother, Vanessa spends as much time as possible doing "mom things" with her children.

mom working in a small, rundown Texas studio owned by John Burnett (Kris Kristofferson). When Burnett hires Cuban-born Rafael (Chayanne) as a studio handyman, Ruby and Rafael begin dancing together and soon fall in love.

Although the film did not receive glowing reviews from critics, Vanessa was singled out for praise. *The New York Times* critic Stephen Holden wrote: "The film's happiest surprise is the uninhibited performance of Vanessa L. Williams . . . [She]

explodes joyously to life. . . . Ms. Williams happens to
be a superb dancer who consistently eclipses her
costar in versatility, grace, and *joie de vivre*." In addition to acting and dancing in the film, Vanessa and
Chayanne recorded a duet for the soundtrack called
"You Are My Home."

In 1998, the star of stage, screen, and music was
the latest in a long line of celebrities to sport a milk
mustache for the famous "Milk: Where's Your Mustache?" advertising campaign. Vanessa's ad, showing
her in a recording studio, debuted in the June 29,
1998, issue of *USA Today*. Kurt Graetzer, executive
director of The Milk Processor Education Program
said, "Vanessa Williams is a great role model to
emphasize the importance of drinking milk."

In her next project, Vanessa joined popular
singer-actor Mandy Patinkin, puppet stars Elmo,
Bert, Ernie, Big Bird, and the rest of the *Sesame Street*
cast for the Columbia Pictures children's film *Elmo in
Grouchland*. Shot in Wilmington, North Carolina,
the plot follows Elmo as he stumbles into a faraway
land inhabited by rude, grouchy, trash-loving crea-
tures, with Vanessa appearing as their "Queen of
Trash." As soon as filming was complete, Vanessa
was at work on the set of the ABC made-for-TV
movie *Future Sport*, costarring Wesley Snipes and
Dean Cain.

Today, Vanessa is more sure of her career moves.
She spoke to a *Toronto Sun* reporter about her work:
"I used to get defensive. I used to say 'I've always been
this talented. You just didn't give me the chance!'
Now, I still get upset about a lot of things, like other
people, but it's the way you handle them that makes
you who you are. Deal with it, move on, and release it."

One way Vanessa releases the negativity that
comes from a life lived in the media spotlight is
through her hobbies. She likes to ride horses, roller-
skate, go to the movies, and exercise. Her exercise
routine includes a machine named after Joseph H.

Pilates (pronounced Pi-lah-tees). Pilates developed a style of body conditioning using a specialized exercise machine with a six- or seven-foot bed that slides back and forth with springs and pulleys. The motion of the exercise is similar to rowing a boat. The Pilates Method was originally designed for injured dancers to rehabilitate their muscles. Vanessa says it is the best way for her to lose inches but not build bulk.

When she is not working, Vanessa insists that she is just another mom, dressed in jeans and sneakers with her hair pulled back, shuttling the kids to school and their various lessons. Three days a week, she takes her older daughter, Melanie, to a Mommy and Me class where they join other kids and moms for gym, music, and dance lessons. During the day, Vanessa either records or practices dance until the kids come home from school in the afternoon. After homework and dinner, she likes to read. As a big fan of self-help and New Age books, one of her favorites is a book on *deng shui,* the Asian practice of placing objects and designing rooms and buildings to best engender happiness and prosperity. Among deng shui's many rules of placement is the use of plants to boost mood. It also claims that placing a bed near a window, but not facing the door, is crucial for leaving behind the problems of the outside world.

Vanessa enjoys making lists of her future goals. "OK, it's a New Age thing," she admitted, "but it helps me get it out of my system." What's on her list right now? "Sometimes I'm just thanking God for the blessings in my life and for guiding my children. I wouldn't object if movie musicals came back into style. If they did, I could be in luck."

Another of Vanessa's New Age beliefs is that family birth order affects one's personality. "The oldest child is very productive and responsible, the middle child is the compromiser and peacemaker, and the baby— well, the baby is the fun-loving, doted-upon baby!" In describing how the birth-order phenomenon

applied to her failed marriage with Hervey, Vanessa found that it revealed a lot about their problems. "The relationship with my husband was very goal-oriented," she said. "We were two oldest children together, so there were two people used to being in control, and neither one was comfortable with taking a backseat. In my new relationship, there is more give-and-take and less struggle for control and power, like you tend to get when you share the same birth order."

Vanessa is still dating Christopher Solimine, whom she met while filming *The Odyssey*. Solimine spends much of his free time with Vanessa and her children, and she is discreet but enthusiastic about

Singing with Luciano Pavarotti, Vanessa and the famed tenor warm up at a dress rehearsal for their performance on Saturday Night Live's 1998 Christmas show.

The audience reaches out to Vanessa as she performs onstage. The loyalty and support of her fans has been one of Vanessa's mainstays during the bright side and the dark side of her career.

the relationship. "I'm much more assertive in a relationship now. I ask for what I need and I am able to give it back. I'm very happy with the situation."

That sentiment also extends to other aspects of Vanessa's life. "The kids are happy and adjusted. I feel great. I'm picking and choosing what I really want to do careerwise, not just working to have something to do." Like many working moms, she wishes there were more hours in the day, but she has no plans of slowing down her career. "The pull between being a mom and having a career is never in balance," she lamented. "You always wish you were there. And when you are devoting time to your family, there is the pressure of making money, keeping this well-oiled machine running, which means you have to get out there and work. So the juggling act never stops." She claims to have set the same goals for her children that her parents set for her. "I want them to be educated, grounded, and well-rounded individuals," she said. "I want them to have great life experiences. But most of all, I want each of them to have a happy life."

Although she hopes that none of her children are forced to go through the public humiliation that she endured, the years have given Vanessa the chance to realize that she grew from her negative experiences. "It was definitely a huge life lesson that I had to carve my way through. But after having done that at 20, I feel like I can handle almost anything," she explained. When so many people thought she could not recover from the scandal, it only made her more determined to be a success. "[P]eople who said that didn't know me," she added. "My family, and the people who sweated next to me in dance class and performed with me in shows over the years all said to me, 'When the dust settles, you'll get the last laugh.' And I knew it was only a matter of time. You can call that being arrogant or cocky, but I knew I'd get a shot. And the more shots I got, the more people said, 'Oh, I didn't know she could do that.' At first, you get defensive and say, 'Of course I can do that. There's so much more to me than what's been in the paper.' Now I know that you'll have your fans, and some people will never be among them."

About her professional future, Vanessa has said, "My philosophy is that you get a chance to be rewarded if you do good. I definitely like the variety of my career and hope it never goes away." Projects currently in negotiation for Vanessa include the story of Sally Hemmings, Thomas Jefferson's black slave mistress, and an adaptation of *The Blue Angel*, the movie that made German actress Marlene Dietrich a star. "Finally, I have a choice of great, diverse roles," Vanessa exclaimed. "There are black women stars now who are making money and who are bringing monies in. It doesn't have to be just a black film. Black women can be in any kind of situation."

Vanessa Williams has indeed proven that she can handle any situation. The 36-year-old film, stage, and recording star has endured more than her share of triumphs and tribulations. She has survived the humiliation of having the crown and title of Miss America taken away from her and triumphed by proving she has the talent, guts, and resolve to overcome scandal and disappointment. In Vanessa's case, success has been the best revenge.

CHRONOLOGY

1963   Vanessa Lynn Williams is born to Helen and Milton Williams in The Bronx, New York, on March 18

1964   Family moves to Millwood, New York

1967   Brother, Christopher, is born

1980   Graduates from Horace Greeley High School, Chappaqua, New York

1981   Enters Syracuse University, majoring in musical theater

1982   Works for Tom Chiapel as a receptionist, makeup artist, and model; poses nude for Chiapel

1983   Wins titles Miss Greater Syracuse, Miss New York State, and Miss America 1984

1984   Forced to resign Miss America title because provocative photos of her appear in *Penthouse*

1987   Marries Ramon Hervey; relocates to California

1988   Daughter Melanie is born; releases first album, *The Right Stuff*; the album goes gold, with more than 600,000 copies sold and is nominated for three Grammy Awards; wins NAACP Award for Best New Female Artist

1990   Daughter Jillian is born

1991   Hosts *The Soul of VH-1*; releases second album, *The Comfort Zone*; the album goes platinum and is nominated for a Grammy Award

1992   Single "Save the Best for Last" tops the charts for six weeks

1993   Sings "Save the Best for Last" at inauguration of President Bill Clinton; son Devin is born

1994   Releases third album, *The Sweetest Days*; replaces Chita Rivera as star of *Kiss of the Spider Woman* on Broadway; moves back to the East Coast with family

1995   Stars in television remake of *Bye Bye Birdie*; separates from husband

1996   Single "Colors of the Wind," from the *Pocahontas* soundtrack wins Academy Award for Best Song; co-stars with Arnold Schwarzenegger in blockbuster hit *Eraser*; fourth album, *Star Bright*, is released

1997   Divorces Ramon Hervey after 10 years of marriage; stars in films *Hoodlum* and *Soul Food*; releases fifth album, *Next*

1998   Recieves NAACP Image Award as Outstanding Actress in a Motion Picture for her role in *Soul Food*; appears at city center in concert version of *St. Louis Woman*; film *Dance with Me* is released; films *Elmo in Grouchland* and *Future Sport*; greatest hits album is released

1999   Marries basketball player Rick Fox; appears in film *Light It Up*; serves as narrator for television miniseries *I'll Make Me A World*

2000   Stars in television movies *The Courage to Love* and *Don Quixote*; appears on the big screen in *Shaft*; gives birth to daughter Sasha Gabriella

THE ROAD TO MISS AMERICA

There is something about that magical moment when the glittering tiara is placed upon the head of the new Miss America that sparks a fantasy in millions of young girls. Although Vanessa Williams only entered a handful of pageants before becoming Miss America, most winners of the crown have worked for years to achieve their goal.

The pageant industry is a big business. Each year, thousands of contestants from all over the country enter local preliminary pageants. These local pageants remain largely rural attractions and are usually not held in big cities. At the Miss America Pageant, less than one-fifth of the competitors come from the nation's 25 largest cities (where more than one-third of the U.S. population resides). In many small towns, the local Miss America qualifying contest is considered the social event of the year. The 2,000 or so local competitions are the first step along the road to the crown. Civic groups, such as the Jaycees or Junior Citizens, are authorized to conduct official preliminary competitions in their communities. Each local franchise is then required to conduct its operation in accordance with pageant regulations to ensure a uniform standard of quality.

Prospective contestants either hear about the pageant through advertisements, word of mouth, or by writing or calling the pageant's national office for assistance. The staff directs inquiries to state pageant officials who, in turn, will put a contestant in touch with a regional or local director in their community.

After locating a preliminary contest in her area and contacting pageant organizers, the contestant then begins the application process. At her request, an information packet containing the pageant's rules and regulations, along with an application form, is sent to the contestant. The contestant is asked to fill out the entry form and return it with several photographs. These pictures offer judges their first glimpse of the candidate.

If she is accepted as a contestant, the young woman receives a detailed schedule of various pageant events. The kickoff to a local pageant traditionally involves a party and an orientation meeting at which each entrant meets the pageant volunteers with whom she will be working. Weekly rehearsals are usually held in a local school auditorium with a dress rehearsal staged the night before the pageant.

The morning of the pageant, the first competitive event, the private interview, is conducted at a local community college or hotel conference room. These private conversations between judges and contestants last about seven minutes and are scheduled a few minutes apart to allow panelists time to award scores and reorganize their notes in preparation for the next candidate. After the interview, contestants begin to prepare for the evening's competition.

On pageant night, the program begins with an opening production number followed by an introduction of the judges and an acknowledgment of the sponsors. The reigning titleholder is presented to the audience. Then the competition begins.

At the end of the last event, the evening-gown competition, contestants remain in their gowns and are escorted on stage to await the panel's announcement of the new winner. Once the tabulations are complete, the reigning queen delivers her farewell speech. Then comes the moment everyone has been waiting for—the announcement of which candidate will wear the local crown and represent her community in the state finals.

The master of ceremonies dramatically announces the name of the new local titleholder, while the audience wonders if the woman they are applauding will become their state titleholder or perhaps even the next Miss America.

Once the winner has been chosen, she has a brief orientation and a judges' critique. The critique is a private meeting at which the judges give the winner feedback on her performance and offer suggestions for the upcoming state pageant. Most new titleholders are eager to listen to the panel's expert advice.

The months leading up to the state competition are filled with public appearances, parades, style shows, and social and business gatherings. Local winners may even attend other preliminaries to meet some of her competitors. In order to gain more poise, state contestants are encouraged to speak in public as often as possible. At her appearances, a titleholder is always accompanied by a responsible chaperone and/or official hostess to ensure her safety and well-being. Public appearances often involve a modest fee and travel expenses. Hotels and meals are paid for by the organizations requesting the contestant's presence or by the pageant franchise.

With the state pageant a few months away, preparations are well under way: Flattering photos are taken for the judges; competition wardrobe is chosen; and contestants practice their talent and ability to handle difficult questions for the interview segment. With so much to do, the key to approaching a state competition with confidence is to prepare thoroughly in every area before taking off for pageant week.

Each year, 2,000 local titleholders from across the country train and groom in anticipation of the upcoming state competitions—where 50 young women (one from each state) will take a step farther down the road toward the goal of the Miss America title.

State pageants are traditionally conducted in late spring and early summer, depending upon the size of the state and the number of participants. Smaller state programs, such as those in the New England states, including Connecticut, Rhode Island, Massachusetts, New Hampshire, Vermont, and Maine, may have a dozen contestants, while larger programs like Miss Utah and Miss Texas pageants, may have 60 or more participants. Because of differences in size, state pageant schedules vary from one-day contests to week-long competitions.

State competitions are especially popular in the southern states. In Arkansas, where interest in pageants is high, more than 200 volunteers help coordinate the state pageant. In many states, the schedule is designed to duplicate the national pageant schedule in order to prepare the eventual winner for the demands of national competition. Miss Arkansas pageant director, Bob Wheeler, said they use the same system that is used in Atlantic City, "So when Miss Arkansas goes to Miss America, the schedule is the very same thing she experienced here in Arkansas. It's just on a bigger scale."

In many areas of the country, pageants are telecast live statewide. As the week of competition ends and the contestants await the judges' verdict, each one yearns to have her name announced as her state's representative to the Miss America Pageant. The moment of victory arouses a flood of sentiments for the winner—pride at having reached a difficult goal, excitement that the national pageant lies just a few months down the road, even relief that the pressure of the state pageant is over.

The state judges' critiques, just as important as those conducted on the local level, always supply the winner with constructive advice for improvement during the national competition.

The entire focus of the first few months of a state queen's reign is directed toward preparing her for the upcoming Miss America Pageant, which is in mid-September. The new titleholder is introduced to her business manager and the team of volunteers that will help her prepare for the national competition. Then they get to work again.

While the Miss America Pageant attracts a loyal television audience and has spawned a succession of imitators, it manages to survive with limited financial resources and meager yearly revenues The pageant relies solely on the work of a team of 200,000 volunteers across the country. Even during the complicated scheduling and coordination of the Miss America Pageant week in Atlantic City, activities for the 50 contestants are arranged by 400 generous volunteers. Despite its low level of financing, the pageant has a waiting list of large and profitable corporations that want to link their products with Miss America's wholesome, all-American image.

While the pageant was originally created to boost the economy of Atlantic City, it no longer turns big profits for the shore community. In a city fortified by gambling, the crush of beauty-contest followers does little more than make hotel rooms scarce. The Chamber of Commerce has estimated that the pageant pumps about $10 million into the resort's economy each year. That is less than the casinos take in from gamblers on a good day.

But the tearful crowning of Miss America does provide another type of payoff for the gambling mecca. "It brings to the resort a wholesome, family atmosphere. It's an image builder rather than a tourist attraction. Nobody, including the casinos, wants Atlantic City to be known as a gambling town," said the senior vice president of Caesar's Boardwalk Regency Hotel.

With the exception of the women who have used the Miss America crown to springboard their careers as performers, including Phyllis George, Mary Ann Mobley, Lee Meriwether, and Vanessa Williams, Miss America eventually fades from the limelight after her reign is complete. But the joy of being crowned and the memories of traveling all over the country remain.

Besides Vanessa's success as an actress and singer, Miss America 1955, Lee Meriwether starred with Buddy Ebsen in the popular television series *Barnaby Jones*. Phyllis George, Miss America 1971, became the first female sportscaster on television. "[A]ll survivors are winners," George said. "[A]nd the Miss America Pageant is one fabulous winner!" Mary Ann Mobley, Miss America 1959, is now married to the pageant's host, Gary Collins. She has written and produced television documentaries, in addition to her work on various charity boards in her home state of California. Mobley said, "The pageant will . . . last as long as the local and state volunteers have the will to devote all the time and energy it takes to send great contestants to Atlantic City."

After more than 75 years as the most well-known and prestigious of beauty pageants, Miss America will continue to make young girls dream and even make some lucky young women's dreams come true.

ACCOMPLISHMENTS

ALBUMS

The Right Stuff (1988)
The Comfort Zone (1991)
The Sweetest Days (1994)
Star Bright (1996)
Next (1997)
Vanessa Williams's Greatest Hits—The First Ten Years (1998)

MUSICAL APPEARANCES

Soul Train, Live!
Dick Clark Presents
Club MTV
Live at the Improv
Video Soul (Black entertainment television)

FILMS

The Pick Up Artist (1987)
Under the Gun (1989)
Harley Davidson and the Marlboro Man (1991)
Another You (1991)
Eraser (1996)
Hoodlum (1997)
Soul Food (1997)
Dance With Me (1998)
Elmo in Grouchland (1998)
Light It Up (1999)
Shaft (2000)

THEATER

The Courage to Love (2000)
Don Quixote (2000)

TELEVISION APPEARANCES

Partners in Crime (1984)
He's the Mayor (1986)
Full Exposure: The Sex Tapes Scandal (1989)
The Kid Who Loved Christmas (1990)
Perry Mason: The Case of the Silenced Singer (1990)
The Jacksons: An American Dream (1992)
Stompin' at the Savoy (1992)
Sidney Sheldon's Nothing Lasts Forever (1995)
Bye Bye Birdie (1995)
The Odyssey (1997)
Future Sport (1998)
I'll Make Me A World (1999)
The Courage to Love (2000)
Don Quixote (2000)

BIBLIOGRAPHY

Bivans, Ann-Marie. *Miss America in Pursuit of the Crown*. New York: MasterMedia Limited, 1991.

"Black Leaders Praise Choice of First Black Miss America." *The New York Times*, September 19, 1983.

Brady, James. "Vanessa Williams." *Parade Magazine*, December 3, 1995.

Brantley, Ben. "The Birthright of Beauty: Free and Easy." *The New York Times*, 1998.

Brown, Tony. "Miss America Undressed." *Tony Brown's Journal*, July/September 1994.

Chira, Susan. "First Black Miss America Finds Unforeseen Issues." *The New York Times*, April 3, 1984.

Cunningham, Kim. "Let Us Entertain You." *People Weekly*, July 1996.

Darling, Lynn. "The Comeback Queen." *Harper's Bazaar*, July 1994.

Eady, Brenda. "She's Black and Miss America, But Vanessa Williams Is Most of All Her Own Woman." *People Weekly*, October 3, 1983.

Ebert, Alan. "'I'm A Fighter.'" *Parade Magazine*, June 16, 1996.

Fein, Esther B. "Flowers, Love and Offers of Help Await Miss America at Her Home." *The New York Times*, July 22, 1984.

Gregory, Deborah. "Vanessa Williams." *Essence*, July 1996.

"Home Early, a Miss America Ponders an Unsettled Future." *The New York Times*, September 1, 1984.

"In New York: The Miss Is a Hit." *Time*, October 17, 1983.

Janson, Donald. "Miss America Asked To Quit Over Photos Showing Her Nude." *The New York Times*, July 21, 1984.

Johnson, Robert E. ""Vanessa." *Jet*, August 1, 1994.

Kahn, Sheryl. ""Vanessa Erasing the Past." *McCall's*, July 1996.

McGuigan, Cathleen, and Jennifer Boeth. "Miss America: A Title Lost." *Newsweek*, July 30, 1984.

McLaughlin, Peter, and Ruth Landa. "Vanessa: Pix were private." *Daily News*, July 23, 1984.

Morgan, Joan, and Audrey Edwards. "Vanessa Williams." *Essence*, August 1994.

Newman, Bruce. "I, Calypso." *TV Guide*, May 17, 1997.

Norment, Lynn. "Here She Is . . . Miss America." *Ebony*, December 1983.

Norment, Lynn. "Vanessa Williams on her painful divorce, the pressures of superstardom, and her new life as a single mom." *Ebony*, October 1997.

Osborne, Angela Saulino. *Miss America: The Dream Lives On*. Dallas: Taylor Publishing Company, 1995.

Pacheco, Patrick. "Dream Girl: Vanessa Williams Hits Broadway and Realizes a Childhood Fantasy." *FanFare*, July 10, 1994.

Rudolph, Ileane. "The fall and rise of Vanessa Williams: dethroned Miss America is now back on the fast track." *TV Guide*, May 18, 1991.

Smith, Danyel. "Sweet Revenge." *US*, January 1995.

"Vanessa's Family Pride." *Daily News*, December 18, 1994.

"Vanessa Williams, Arnold Schwarzenegger Star In Thriller 'Eraser.'" *Jet*, June 10, 1996.

"Vanessa Williams: A Thorny Crown Goes with the Job of Being the First Black Miss America." *People Weekly*, December 26, 1983–January 2, 1984.

"Vanessa Williams's Extraordinary Comeback." *McCall's*, April 1992.

Waldron, Clarence. "Vanessa Williams." *Jet*, January 16, 1995.

Whitaker, Charles. "A New Life for Vanessa." *Ebony*, April 1987.

"Williams Reports She Posed for other Nude Photographs." *The New York Times*, August 24, 1984.

Wohlfert-Wihlborg, Lee. "Here She Comes . . ." *People Weekly*, September 19, 1983.

INDEX

PICTURE CREDITS

SUZANNE FREEDMAN is a former librarian with a penchant for biographies. She has written on the chief justices of the Supreme Court, as well as primatologist Dian Fossey, civil rights activist Ida B. Wells-Barnett, and Secretary of State Madeleine K. Albright. *Vanessa Williams* is her ninth book.

NATHAN IRVIN HUGGINS, one of America's leading scholars in the field of black studies, helped select the titles for the BLACK AMERICANS OF ACHIEVEMENT series, for which he also served as senior consulting editor. He was the W. E. B. DuBois Professor of History and Afro-American Studies at Harvard University and the director of the W. E. B. DuBois Institute for Afro-American Research at Harvard. He received his doctorate from Harvard in 1962 and returned there as professor in 1980 after teaching at Columbia University, the University of Massachusetts, Lake Forest College, and the California State University, Long Beach. He was the author of four books and dozens of articles, including *Black Odyssey: The Afro-American Ordeal in Slavery*, *The Harlem Renaissance*, and *Slave and Citizen: The Life of Frederick Douglass*, and was associated with the Children's Television Workshop, National Public Radio, the Boston Athenaeum, the Museum of Afro-American History, the Howard Thurman Educational Trust, and Upward Bound. Professor Huggins died in 1989, at the age of 62, in Cambridge, Massachusetts.